RESILIENT
SUSTAINABLE ARCHITECTURE

© 2024 Instituto Monsa de ediciones.

First edition in September 2024 by Monsa Publications,
Carrer Gravina 43 (08930) Sant Adrià de Besós.
Barcelona (Spain)
T +34 93 381 00 93
www.monsa.com
monsa@monsa.com

Editor and Project director Anna Minguet
Art Director: Layout and Cover Design
Eva Minguet (Monsa Publications)
Printed in Spain
Shop online:
www.monsashop.com

Follow us!
Instagram: @monsapublications

ISBN: 978-84-17557-78-2
B 11164-2024

All rights reserved. No part of this book may be used or reproduced in any manner whatsoever without written permission except in the case of brief quotations embodied in critical articles and reviews. Whole or partial reproduction of this book without the editor's authorisation infringes reserved rights; any utilization must be previously requested.

"Queda prohibida, salvo excepción prevista en la ley, cualquier forma de reproducción, distribución, comunicación pública y transformación de esta obra sin contar con la autorización de los titulares de propiedad intelectual. La infracción de los derechos mencionados puede ser constitutiva de delito contra la propiedad intelectual (Art. 270 y siguientes del Código Penal). El Centro Español de Derechos Reprográficos (CEDRO) vela por el respeto de los citados derechos".

RESILIENT SUSTAINABLE ARCHITECTURE

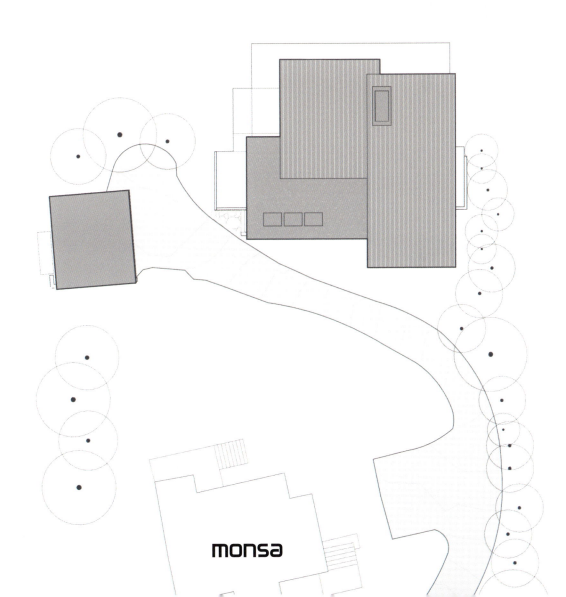

monsa

Introducción INTRO

En un mundo cada vez más consciente de los desafíos ambientales y sociales, la arquitectura sostenible y resiliente emerge como un faro de esperanza y progreso. Esta disciplina no solo aborda las necesidades actuales de la sociedad, sino que también se anticipa y prepara para los desafíos del futuro.

La arquitectura sostenible busca crear entornos construidos que minimicen su impacto negativo en el medio ambiente, utilizando recursos de manera eficiente, reduciendo la huella de carbono y promoviendo la conservación y regeneración de los ecosistemas naturales. A través de la integración de tecnologías innovadoras y prácticas de diseño inteligentes, los arquitectos pueden crear edificios que consuman menos energía, utilicen materiales renovables y fomenten un estilo de vida más saludable y equilibrado para sus ocupantes.

Por otro lado, la arquitectura resiliente se centra en la capacidad de los edificios y comunidades para resistir y recuperarse de eventos extremos, como desastres naturales, crisis económicas o cambios climáticos repentinos. Al anticipar y mitigar los riesgos, los arquitectos pueden diseñar estructuras que sean más seguras, adaptables y capaces de mantener la funcionalidad y la habitabilidad incluso en condiciones adversas.

Este libro reúne las obras de arquitectos y estudios que abrazan y promueven estos principios de sostenibilidad y resiliencia en su trabajo. A través de una variedad de proyectos inspiradores y visionarios, exploramos cómo la arquitectura puede ser una fuerza positiva para el cambio, transformando no solo nuestros entornos construidos, sino también nuestra relación con el mundo natural y entre nosotros mismos.

Esta nueva arquitectura, con visión de futuro, más sostenible y resiliente, se convierte en una herramienta poderosa para construir un mundo mejor para las generaciones presentes y futuras.

In an increasingly conscious world of environmental and social challenges, sustainable and resilient architecture emerges as a beacon of hope and progress. This discipline not only addresses the current needs of society but also anticipates and prepares for the challenges of the future.

Sustainable architecture seeks to create built environments that minimize their negative impact on the environment by using resources efficiently, reducing carbon footprint, and promoting conservation and regeneration of natural ecosystems. Through the integration of innovative technologies and intelligent design practices, architects can create buildings that consume less energy, use renewable materials, and foster a healthier and more balanced lifestyle for their occupants.

On the other hand, resilient architecture focuses on the ability of buildings and communities to withstand and recover from extreme events such as natural disasters, economic crises, or sudden climate changes. By anticipating and mitigating risks, architects can design structures that are safer, more adaptable, and capable of maintaining functionality and habitability even under adverse conditions.

This book brings together the works of architects and studios that embrace and promote these principles of sustainability and resilience in their work. Through a variety of inspiring and visionary projects, we explore how architecture can be a positive force for change, transforming not only our built environments but also our relationship with the natural world and with each other.

This new architecture, with a future-oriented, more sustainable, and resilient vision, becomes a powerful tool for building a better world for present and future generations.

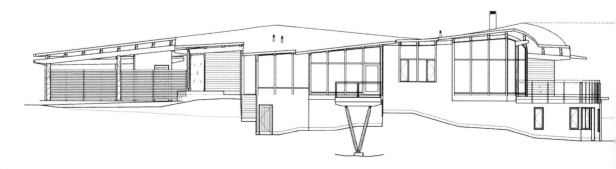

Índice INDEX

ISLAND RETREAT	10
MAZAMA HOUSE	18
PUSH PULL HOUSE	24
SEAVIEW ESCAPE	30
HIGH DESERT MODERN	38
TREE HOUSE	46
COURTYARD HOUSE ON A RIVER	52
CANNON BEACH RESIDENCE	56
LIVE EDGE RESIDENCE	62
GLASS BOX	68
OAK GROVE HOUSE	76
SOLAR CREST HOUSE	82
RIDGE HOUSE	90
CANYON SHELTER	96
ROCKRIDGE	102
DANCING LIGHT RESIDENCE	108
MOD.FAB	116
ALTA LUZ	120
FRIO RANCH	128
CARVE HOUSE	134

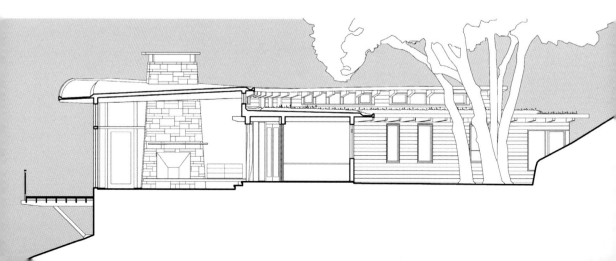

ISLAND RETREAT

Bainbridge Island, Washington // Lot area: 21,780 sq ft; building area: 2,600 sq ft

Este refugio de dos dormitorios en la ladera de la colina permite a la familia disfrutar de una escapada a la isla de forma habitual. Los suelos de madera y el amplio acristalamiento de las dos plantas ofrecen una vista de las montañas desde el balcón superior. Los peldaños de la escalera de madera en voladizo conducen a una biblioteca con vistas al salón y a un comedor de doble altura en la parte inferior. Los motivos playeros y las lámparas náuticas, elegidas para los baños, aportan una sensación costera al interior. Un muro de piedra con paneles de acero Corten es el centro de atención del salón, que alberga una chimenea y un centro multimedia, a la vez que separa la suite principal. Un camino arbolado conecta la casa con la playa, creando una transición natural entre la vivienda y el exterior. Un camino común, compartido por los dos refugios, ofrece una vista única del tejado verde en voladizo.

This two-bedroom hillside retreat allows the family to enjoy a regular island getaway. Wood floors and expansive two-story glazing bestow a view of the mountains from the upper balcony. Cantilevered wood "floating" stair treads lead to a library overlooking the double-height living and dining spaces below. Beach glass and nautical light fixtures, chosen for the bathrooms, bring a coastal feel indoors. A stone mass wall with Corten panels provides the focal point of the living space, housing a fireplace and media center while providing separation from the master suite. A wooded pathway connects the home to the beach, creating a natural transition from home to the outdoors. A communal drive, shared between the two siblings' retreat homes, provides a unique overlook of the cantilevered green roof.

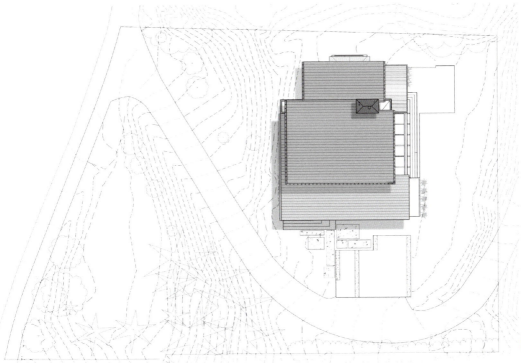

Site plan

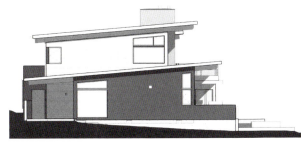

South elevation

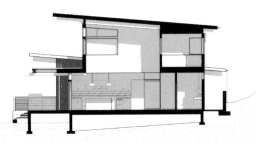

Section through dining area and guest bedroom

East elevation

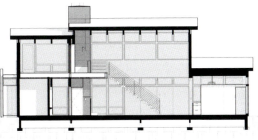

Section through staircase

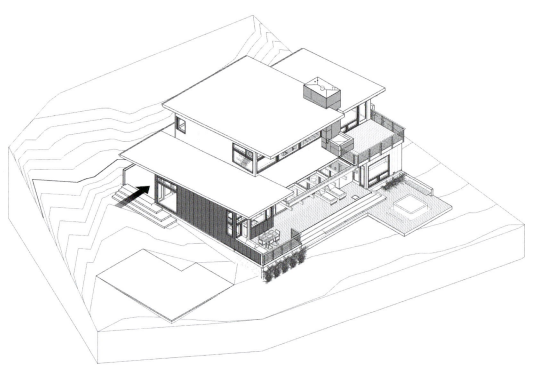

Axonometric view

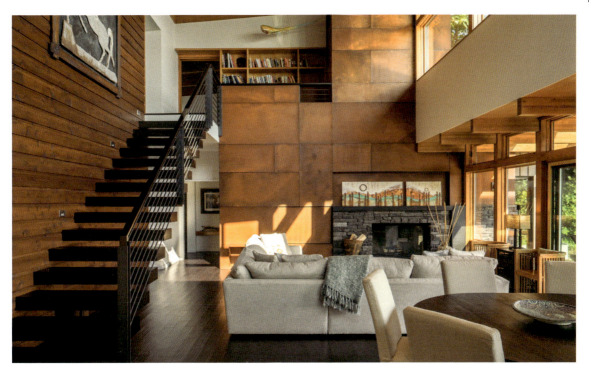

Ground floor plan

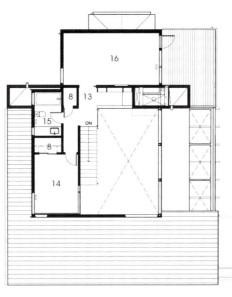

Second floor plan

1. Entry
2. Powder room
3. Mud/laundry room
4. Kitchen
5. Dining area
6. Living area
7. Office
8. Closet
9. Master bedroom
10. Master bathroom
11. Master closet
12. Mechanical room
13. Library
14. Bedroom
15. Bathroom
16. Media room

MAZAMA HOUSE

Winthrop, Washington, United States // Lot area: 4 acres; building area: 4,300 sq ft

La casa está situada en un bosquecillo de árboles en el extremo oriental de una gran pradera en el borde oriental de las Cascadas del Norte. Dos volúmenes de construcción indican la organización de la casa. Un ala de dormitorios de dos pisos ancla un pabellón de estar elevado, levantado del suelo por una serie de columnas de acero expuestas. El nivel de suelo elevado ofrece mejores vistas y mantiene el nivel principal de la vivienda muy por encima de la acumulación de nieve en invierno. La casa refleja la continua investigación de FINNE sobre la idea del modernismo artesanal, con inserciones de bronce fundido en la puerta principal, paneles de barandilla de acero cortados con láser abigarrado, una encimera de cocina curvilínea de vidrio fundido, lámparas de aluminio cortadas con chorro de agua y piezas de mobiliario personalizadas.

The house is located in a copse of trees at the easterly end of a large meadow on the North Cascades' eastern edge. Two building volumes indicate the house organization. A grounded two-story bedroom wing anchors a raised living pavilion, lifted off the ground by a series of exposed steel columns. The raised floor level provides enhanced views and keeps the main living level well above the winter snow accumulation. The house reflects the continuing FINNE investigation into the idea of crafted modernism, with cast bronze inserts at the front door, variegated laser-cut steel railing panels, a curvilinear cast-glass kitchen counter, waterjet-cut aluminum light fixtures, and custom furniture pieces.

PUSH PULL HOUSE

Veneta, Oregon, United States // Lot area: 5.58 acres; building area: 1,500 sq ft

---

El diseño de esta residencia para vigilante relaciona la vivienda pragmática con una conexión psicológica con el mundo natural. Cuatro cuadrados están ensamblados y perforados por ventanas esquineras. La naturaleza es empujada hacia los espacios, mientras que los habitantes se sienten atraídos hacia la naturaleza. Las vistas cambiantes a través de la niebla invernal y las sombras del verano contrastan con la estabilidad interior. Cada espacio se abre a una ventana que aporta luz de todos los lados. Estas aberturas se accionan a distancia para la refrigeración pasiva durante los meses de verano, mientras que la calefacción por losa radiante y una estufa de leña calientan los espacios en invierno. Otras características sostenibles son los muros aislados de 20 cm de grosor, los tejados metálicos y los armarios de abeto Douglas de origen local. La información modelizada de la construcción y los análisis de la ganancia solar lograron un coste de construcción de unos 1720$ por metro cuadrado, lo que redujo en gran medida el uso de energía y permitió un alquiler por debajo del precio del mercado.

The design of this caretaker's residence relates pragmatic habitation with a psychological connection to the natural world. Four squares are assembled and pierced via corner windows. Nature is pushed into the spaces, while the inhabitants feel pulled out toward nature. Changing views through the winter mist and summer shadows is contrasted with the inner stability of the square spaces. Each space rises to a window, bringing in light from all sides. These apertures are operated remotely for passive cooling during the summer months, while radiant slab heating and a wood stove heat the spaces in winter. Other sustainable features include eight-inch-thick insulated walls, metal roofs, and locally-harvested Douglas fir cabinetry. Building information modeling and solar gain analyses achieved a construction cost of $172/sq ft, greatly reducing energy use and allowing below-market-rate rental.

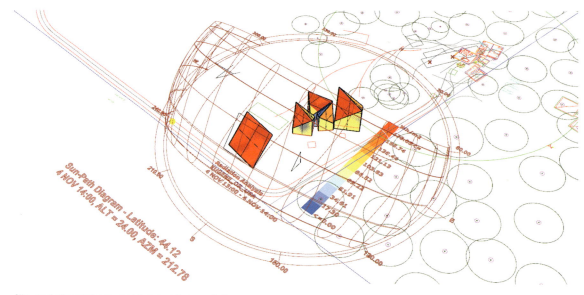

Site and atmosphere, passive cooling parti diagram

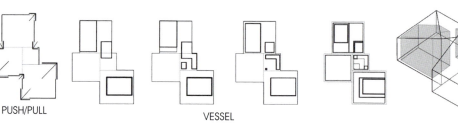

PARTI SPACE PEAKS MONITORS

PUSH/PULL VESSEL VOLUME

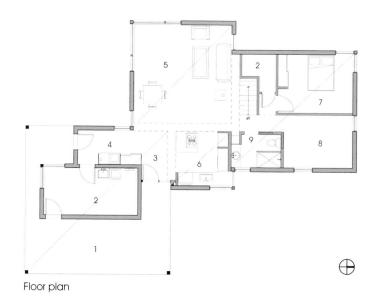

1. Carport
2. Storage
3. Entry
4. Mudroom
5. Living area
6. Kitchen
7. Bedroom
8. Study
9. Bathroom

Floor plan

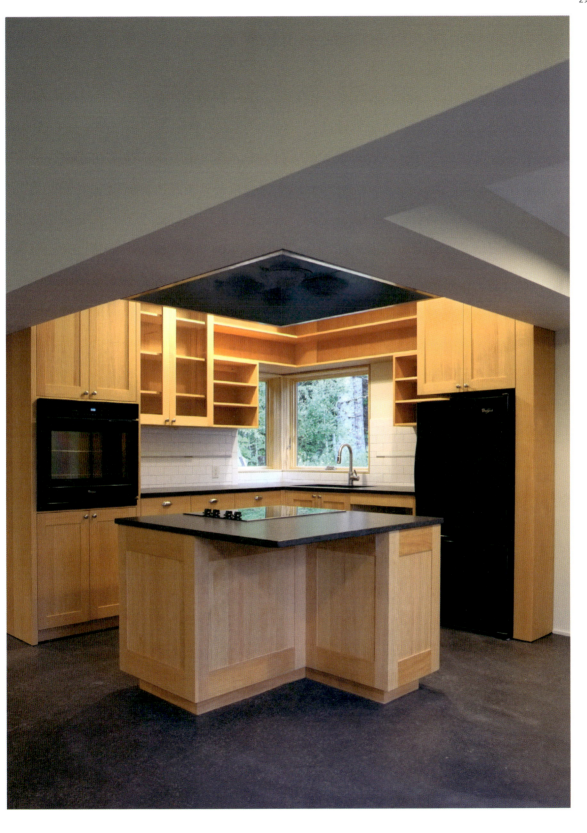

SEAVIEW ESCAPE

Bainbridge Island, Washington, United States // Lot area: 10,890 sq ft; building area: 2,800 sq ft

Esta casa de estilo típico del noroeste del Pacífico está anclada en un terreno con una pendiente pronunciada. Hay un área de sala, comedor y cocina de concepto abierto que se abre directamente al exterior con un sistema de puertas plegables en las esquinas Un muro de masa de piedra divide los espacios públicos y privados de la casa mientras encierra las escaleras, las áreas de apoyo y sala de polvo. Dos hermanos querían un par de casas diseñadas en conjunto en el sitio, con el deseo de usar las casas, a solo 15 metros de distancia, para grandes reuniones familiares. Cada hogar incluye una paleta de materiales de piedra, hormigón, madera y metal, que utilizan la topografía existente y se complementan entre sí al tiempo que definen las diferencias sutiles en los gustos de los hermanos. Un camino de acceso común conduce a las dos casas, proporcionando una vista única del océano y del techo verde.

This shoreline Pacific Northwest-style house is anchored into a steeply sloped site. There is an open-concept living, dining, and kitchen area that opens directly to the outdoors with a corner bi-fold door system. A stone mass wall divides the public and private spaces of the house while enclosing the stairs, support areas, and powder room. Two siblings wanted a pair of homes designed in conjunction with one another on the site, wishing to use the houses—just 50 feet apart—for big family gatherings. Each home includes a material palette of stone, concrete, wood, and metal, utilizes the existing topography, and complements one another while defining the subtle differences in the siblings' tastes. A communal drive leads to the two homes, providing a unique overlook of the ocean and green roof.

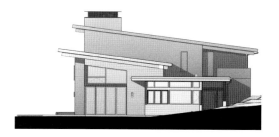
North elevation

South elevation

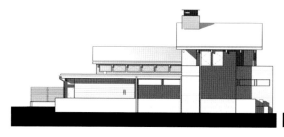
West elevation

East elevation

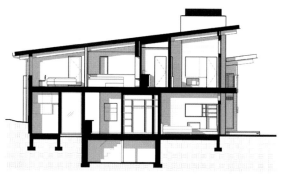
Cross section

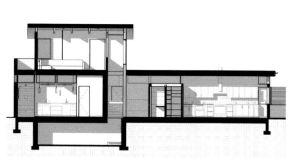
Longitudinal section

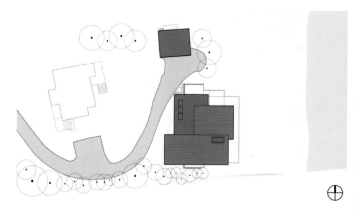
Site plan

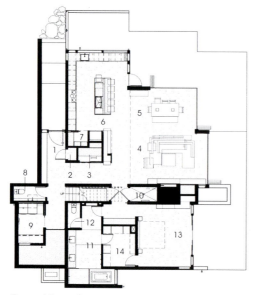

Ground floor plan

Second floor plan

1. Entry
2. Closet
3. Office
4. Family room
5. Dining area
6. Kitchen
7. Pantry
8. Powder room
9. Laundry room
10. Mechanical room
11. Master bathroom
12. Water closet
13. Master bedroom
14. Master closet
15. Staircase
16. Guest bedroom
17. Closet
18. Bathroom
19. Media room
20. Den

HIGH DESERT MODERN

Bend, Oregon, United States // Lot area: .24 acres; building area: 2,670 sq ft (not including garage)

Esta casa en el desierto está diseñada en torno a una serie de espacios llenos de luz que la conectan con el cielo y el paisaje circundantes. Concebida como una navaja suiza, se expande y se contrae para adaptarse al uso de los propietarios, de unos pocos invitados o de grandes reuniones. En el patio de entrada, una mampara enrollable y una puerta batiente cambian el espacio, cómodo y privado o bien abierto y acogedor. La partición entre el salón y la suite principal cuenta con cinco paneles deslizantes que ocultan una chimenea, televisión, almacenamiento y un dormitorio. Una gran pared batiente convierte una sala de estar en un dormitorio de invitados. La paleta exterior mezcla las texturas variadas y los colores sutiles del desierto. En el interior, las líneas limpias y los volúmenes simples y luminosos crean un telón de fondo para las colecciones cambiantes: una fila de máscaras de receptor vintage, engranajes industriales y el tronco de un antiguo lilo.

This desert home is designed around a series of light-filled spaces that connect it to the surrounding sky and landscape. Conceived as a kind of Swiss Army knife, it expands and contracts for use by the owners, a few guests, or large gatherings. At the entry courtyard, a rolling screen and swinging gate can be used to configure the space to be cozy and private or wide open and welcoming. The partition between the living room and main suite features five sliding panels that conceal a fireplace, tv, storage, and bedroom beyond. A large, hinged wall turns a sunny sitting area into a guest bedroom. The exterior palette is designed to blend with the varied textures and subtle colors of the desert. Inside the home's clean lines and simple, light-filled volumes create a backdrop for changing collections: a row of vintage catcher's masks, salvaged industrial gears, and the trunk of an ancient lilac tree.

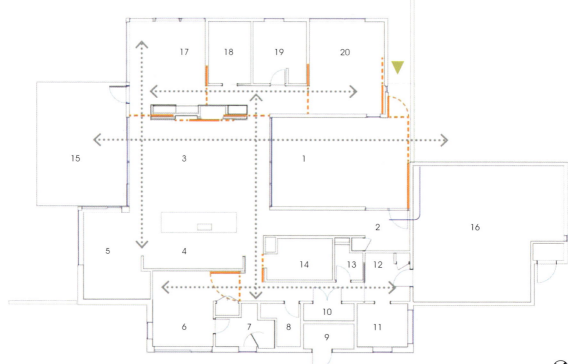

Floor plan

1. Entry courtyard
2. Entry
3. Living area
4. Kitchen/bar
5. Dining area
6. Guest bedroom
7. Guest bathroom
8. Powder room
9. Mechanical room
10. Wine cellar
11. Laundry room
12. Mud room
13. Storage
14. Pantry
15. Patio
16. Garage
17. Master bedroom
18. Master closet
19. Master bathroom
20. Office

TREE HOUSE

Burien, Washington, United States // Lot area: 1.12 acres; building area: 3,800 sq ft (not including garage)

Tree House se alza sobre una parcela arbolada de un acre en la parte superior de un acantilado con vista a Puget Sound. Al principio del proceso de diseño, los clientes, un diseñador gráfico y una artista plástico con dos hijos, describieron el placer que les producía caminar por la propiedad. En respuesta, DA trabajó con ellos para diseñar una casa que brinde diferentes formas de experimentar el sitio, desde habitaciones que están escondidas en la ladera hasta otras que flotan sobre ella. Para el interior, un enfoque de alto contraste para los elementos principales (paredes blancas y una estructura de flexión de acero ennegrecido, suelos de abeto canadiense blanqueados y mobiliario de nogal) atrajo el amor de los clientes por los gráficos fuertes. Elementos como la escalera metalica roja, las superficies de mosaicos gráficos y colores llamativos en todo el mobiliario despiertan una sensación de emoción y de lo inesperado.

Tree House is perched on a one-acre wooded parcel at the top of a bluff overlooking Puget Sound. Early in the design process, the clients—a graphic designer and fine artist with two children—described the pleasure they took in walking the property. In response, DA worked with them to design a home that provides different ways of experiencing the site, from rooms that are tucked into the hillside to others that float above it. For the interior, a high-contrast approach to major elements—white walls and a blackened steel moment frame, bleached hemlock floors, and walnut cabinets—appealed to the clients' love of strong graphics. A sense of delight and the unexpected was introduced through elements such as the red metal stair, fields of graphic tile, and bold colors throughout the furnishings.

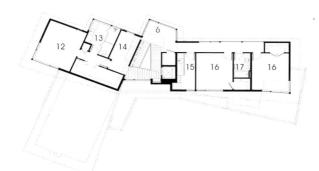

Upper floor plan

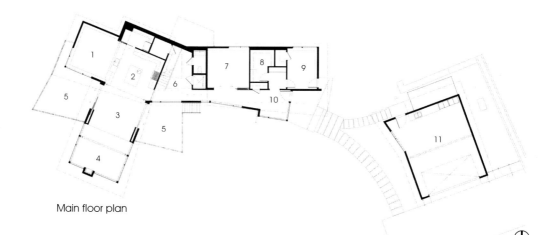

Main floor plan

1. Sunroom
2. Kitchen
3. Dining room
4. Living room
5. Deck
6. Stair hall
7. Family room
8. Mud room
9. Exercise room
10. Entry
11. Garage
12. Master bedroom
13. Master bathroom
14. Office
15. Laundry room
16. Bedroom
17. Bathroom

COURTYARD HOUSE ON A RIVER

Greenwater, Washington, United States // Lot area: 1 acre; building area: 2,000 sq ft

Esta casa se diseñó para una pareja que se trasladó a este lugar rural para disfrutar del esquí y el ciclismo de montaña durante todo el año. Está revestida con una pantalla de lluvia de cedro rojo occidental hecha a medida que se integra en el bosque circundante a lo largo de las orillas del río White, alimentado por glaciares, a la sombra del monte Rainier. Los propietarios actuaron como contratistas y realizaron ellos mismos gran parte del trabajo para mantener un presupuesto de construcción ajustado. El arquitecto y los propietarios/contratistas trabajaron juntos con diligencia durante el proceso de diseño y construcción, y el edificio se mantuvo lo más compacto posible, reduciendo al mínimo la alteración del terreno. Gracias a la planificación de los espacios y las vistas, la iluminación natural cuidadosamente considerada y una paleta de materiales cálidos, la residencia hace hincapié en el diseño.

The home was designed for a couple who relocated to this rural location where they could enjoy skiing and mountain biking year-round. It is clad in a custom-run Western red cedar rainscreen blending into the surrounding forest along the banks of the glacier-fed White River in the shadow of Mount Rainier. The owners served as general contractors and self-performed much of the work to maintain a tight construction budget. With the architect and homeowners/contractors working together diligently throughout the design and construction process, the building was kept as compact as possible, minimizing site disturbance. Through thoughtfully planned spaces and views, carefully considered natural lighting, and a warm material palette, the residence emphasizes design over size.

East elevation West elevation South elevation

Section A Section B

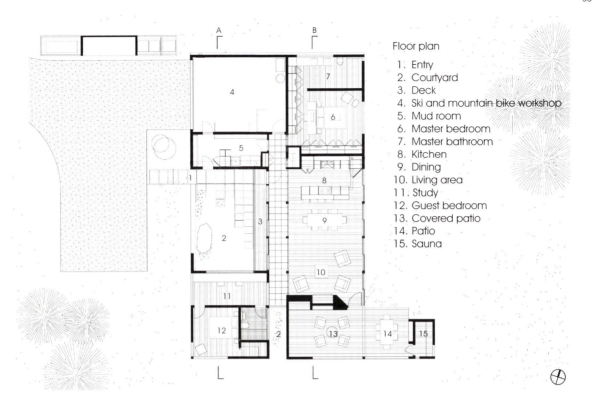

Floor plan
1. Entry
2. Courtyard
3. Deck
4. Ski and mountain bike workshop
5. Mud room
6. Master bedroom
7. Master bathroom
8. Kitchen
9. Dining
10. Living area
11. Study
12. Guest bedroom
13. Covered patio
14. Patio
15. Sauna

CANNON BEACH RESIDENCE

Cannon Beach, Oregon, United States // Lot area: .23 acres; building area: 2,268 sq ft

La Cannon Beach Residence ha servido como refugio para los propietarios, su familia y sus amigos. La casa curvilínea de madera, situada en una ladera boscosa con vistas al Pacífico y al pueblo de Cannon Beach, se centra en las vistas del paisaje circundante y capta el amor de sus propietarios por los materiales y las formas naturales. El diseño, respetuoso con el medio ambiente, fomenta un entorno interior saludable, ofrece una envoltura eficiente y utiliza materiales reciclados para crear un hogar duradero. La Cannon Beach Residence ha recibido numerosos premios, entre ellos el «Custom Green of the Year» de la Asociación Nacional de Constructores de Viviendas, un «Honor Design Award» y un «People's Choice Award» de las secciones de Oregón del Instituto Americano de Arquitectos. En 2019, recibió el premio Stephen Kellert Biophilic Design Award del International Living Futures Institute.

The Cannon Beach Residence has served as a refuge for the owners, their family, and friends. Tucked into a wooded hillside overlooking the Pacific Ocean and the village of Cannon Beach, the curvilinear wood-clad house focuses on the views to the surrounding landscape and captures its owners' love of natural materials and forms. The environmentally responsive design promotes a healthy indoor environment, has an energy-efficient envelope, and utilizes recycled and salvaged materials to create a longlasting home. The Cannon Beach Residence is the recipient of many awards, including the "Custom Green of the Year" by the National Association of Home Builders and an "Honor Design Award" and "People's Choice Award" by the Oregon chapters of the American Institute of Architects. In 2019, it received a Stephen Kellert Biophilic Design Award by the International Living Futures Institute.

Floor plan

1. Entry
2. Guest bedroom
3. Guest bathroom
4. Stairs to loft
5. Kitchen
6. Dining area
7. Living area
8. Stairs to basement
9. Primary bedroom
10. Primary bathroom
11. Garage
12. Utility room
13. Northeast covered porch
14. South covered porch

Section through great room

1. Clean room
2. Kitchen
3. Great room
4. Mechanical room
5. South porch
6. Loft
A. R-30 Durisol Exterior wall-forming system
B. FSC interior framing floors, walls, roof, cabinetry, and formwork
C. Sub-slab rigid insulation
D. Unconditioned "shortened" basement
E. In-line fan coil
F. Hot water storage tanks
G. Heat pump
H. Energy recovery ventilator
I. R-24 Durisol retaining walls
J. Solar-thermal panels
K. Salvaged "windfallen" Incense cedar columns
L. FSC cedar fascia soffits and shakes
M. R-50 insulated roofs
N. Solar-electric panels
O. South-facing clerestory windows
P. Vegetative roof
Q. U= .32 high-performance glazing with cedar frames
R. Clerestory windows
S. Internal thermal-mass stone wall
T. Modified Rumford masonry fireplace

LIVE EDGE RESIDENCE

Bend, Oregon, United States // Lot area: 1.65 acres; building area: 4,150 sq ft

---

Enclavada en un acantilado sobre el pintoresco río Deschutes se encuentra la Live Edge Residencia, con certificación «LEED for Homes Platinum». La casa, con un invernadero anexo, combina una estética de diseño moderno con un intrincado amoldamiento al terreno, tejiendo alrededor de afloramientos rocosos y enebros desgarrados en un árido entorno. Las amplias terrazas exteriores fusionan los espacios interiores con los exteriores y fomentan la vida al aire libre. La Live Edge Residence se diseñó teniendo en cuenta la capacidad de recuperación, lo que permite a los residentes prepararse para lo inesperado. El sistema de baterías Tesla «Power Wall» de 15 kW, la chimenea de leña, la cisterna de agua potable de 1800 litros de agua potable y un invernadero proporcionan una serie de recursos autosuficientes para los ocupantes.

Nestled into a bluff above the scenic Deschutes River sits the LEED for Homes, Platinum-Certified, Live Edge Residence. The house—complete with an attached greenhouse—combines a modern design aesthetic with an intricate molding to the terrain, weaving around rock outcroppings and ragged juniper trees in the arid open-range environment. Extensive exterior terraces merge indoor and outdoor spaces while encouraging outdoor living. Live Edge was designed with resilience in mind, enabling the residents to prepare for the unexpected. The 15 kW Tesla "Power Wall" battery back-up system, wood-burning fireplace, 1,800-gallon potable water cistern, and attached greenhouse provide an array of self-sustaining resources for the occupants.

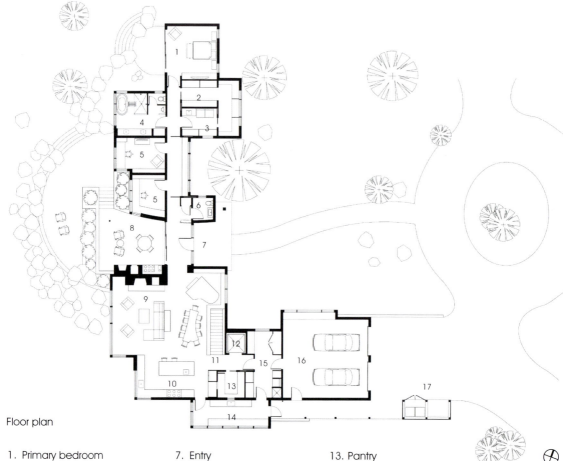

Floor plan

1. Primary bedroom
2. Primary closet
3. Laundry room
4. Primary bathroom
5. Office
6. Guest bathroom
7. Entry
8. Covered patio
9. Great room
10. Kitchen
11. Staircase
12. Elevator
13. Pantry
14. Greenhouse
15. Utility room
16. Garage
17. Firewood

GLASS BOX

San Juan Island, Washington, United States // Lot area: 2.6 acres; building area: 2,744 sq ft

---

Esta casa en lo alto de un promontorio rocoso en la costa de la isla de San Juan está concebida como una joya en las rocas. El estado de la casa existente no se prestaba a una renovación, y los códigos vigentes prohibían una nueva construcción en este extraordinario lugar. En consecuencia, se decidió reutilizar los cimientos existentes, lo que condujo a un enfoque ecológico en el diseño de la nueva casa. La Glass Box se asienta sobre pilares de hormigón que flotan sobre la roca, aprovechando al máximo la luz y las vistas del Canal de San Juan. La yuxtaposición de formas artificiales y naturales se refuerzan mutuamente, preservando la formación de la roca y destacando la configuración arquitectónica de la casa del plano superior. Al oeste, la casa y la de invitados están enclavadas entre los árboles, lo que ofrece un llamativo contraste con la vista abierta y amplia del agua al este.

This home atop a rocky promontory on the shore of San Juan Island is conceived as a jewel on the rock. The condition of the existing house on the site did not lend itself to renovation, and current codes prohibited new construction in this extraordinary location. Consequently, the decision was made to reuse the existing foundations, which led to an environmentally friendly approach in the design of the new home. The Glass Box sits on concrete piers floating above the rock while making the most of the light and views across the San Juan Channel. The juxtaposition of man-made and natural forms reinforce each other, preserving the rock's formation and emphasizing the architectural configuration of the house above. To the west, the house and guest house are nestled among the trees, offering a striking contrast with the open, expansive water view to the east.

Second floor plan

Third floor plan

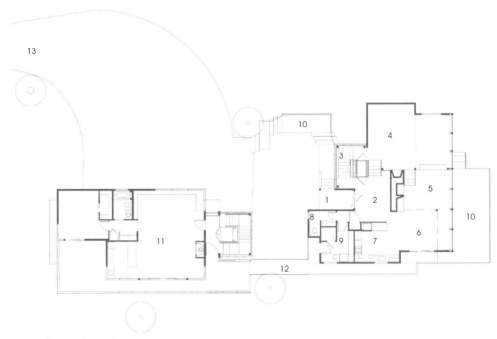

Ground floor plan

1. Covered porch
2. Entry
3. Staircase tower
4. Living room
5. Dining room
6. Sitting room
7. Kitchen
8. Powder room
9. Laundry room
10. Deck
11. Garage and guest house
12. Connecting bridge
13. Driveway
14. Study
15. Master bedroom
16. Sitting area
17. Master bathroom
18. Master closet
19. Open to below
20. Bedroom
21. Bathroom

OAK GROVE HOUSE

Salt Spring Island, British Columbia, Canada // Lot area: 4.57 acres; building area: 2,500 sq ft

La Oak Grove House se diseñó originalmente como un refugio para vivir, asentada serenamente en una hermosa pradera de robles orientada al sur sobre las Islas del Golfo. El equipo de diseño y los constructores tuvieron mucho cuidado en preservar el paisaje natural a lo largo del volumen original y de la construcción de una ampliación una década después. La planta radial de la casa recoge la curva establecida por un robledal de Garry. Su tejado inclinado y ondulado se abre a las vistas del océano y a la luz del sur, mientras que un marco estructural asertivo que incluye columnas de troncos redondos, aporta fuerza visual y calidez al interior. Los revestimientos y las puertas incluyen detalles finos como paneles de cedro con incrustaciones de cobre. Con estos detalles, la belleza de la casa se eleva en respuesta a su glorioso entorno.

Oak Grove House was originally designed as a retreat for living, sitting serenely in a beautiful oak meadow facing south above the Gulf Islands. The design team and builders took great care to preserve the natural landscape throughout the original construction and the building of an extension a decade later. The house's radial plan picks up the curve established by a Garry oak grove. Its tilted and undulating roof opens up to ocean views and south light, while an assertive structural frame—including columns of round logs—imparts visual strength and warmth inside. Siding and doors include such fine details as cedar paneling inset with copper inlay. Finessed with these appointments, the house's beauty rises in response to its glorious setting.

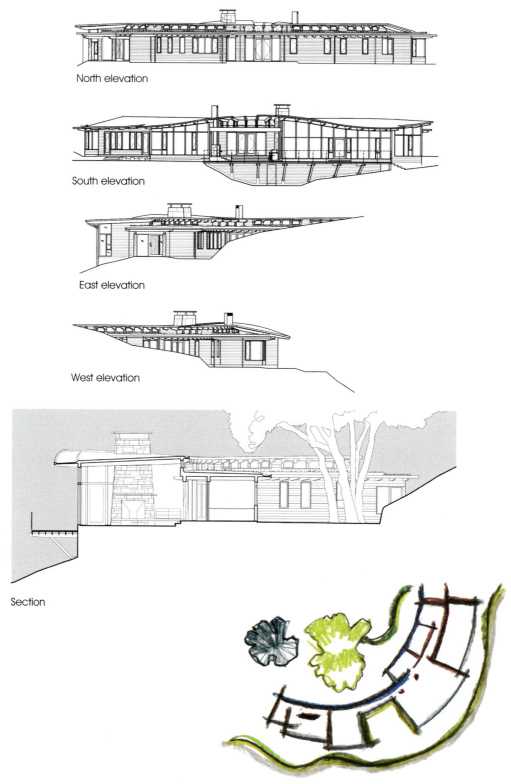

North elevation

South elevation

East elevation

West elevation

Section

Conceptual sketch

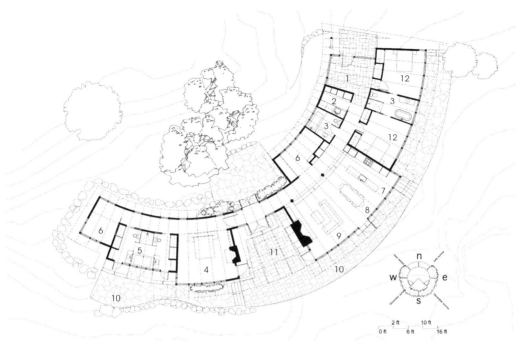

Floor plan

1. Entry
2. Utility/mud room
3. Powder room
4. Main bedroom
5. En suite
6. Den
7. Kitchen
8. Dining area
9. Living area
10. Terrace
11. Outdoor room
12. Bedroom

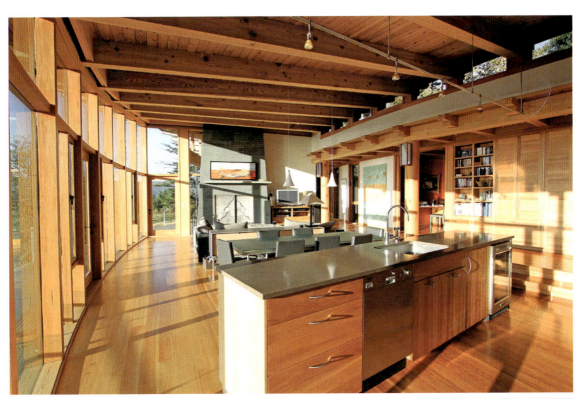

SOLAR CREST HOUSE

Sidney Island, British Columbia, Canada // Lot area: 10 acres; building area: 2,800 sq ft

---

Solar Crest es una casa y un jardín sin conexión a la red eléctrica, que se alza sobre una escarpada cresta rocosa en una remota isla del estrecho de Juan de Fuca. Combina una estudiada formalidad geométrica con elementos orgánicos y sensuales que se funden con el paisaje circundante de granito glaciar redondeado. La planta de la casa es un arco que sigue al sol y a la cresta de la colina, abriéndose a la luz del sur y a las vistas sobre el Estrecho hasta las Montañas Olímpicas del Estado de Washington. En sección, el tejado se ondula, una escultura viva que responde a la jerarquía del uso del espacio, las oportunidades del sol, el aire, las vistas y la forma del propio terreno. Como en la mayoría de los edificios de Blue Sky, la estructura de madera fue la opción de construcción, ya que es relativamente ligera y fácil de mover y utilizar. La mayor parte del abeto y el cedro utilizados en la casa son locales, cosechados y molidos en la cercana isla de Vancouver.

Solar Crest is an off-grid home and garden, embracing a rugged rocky ridge on a remote island in Juan de Fuca Strait. It combines a studied geometric formality with organic and sensuous elements that merge with its surrounding landscape of rounded glaciated granite. The plan of the house is an arc following the sun and the hill's crest opening to southern light and views across the Strait to the Olympic Mountains in Washington State. In section, the roof undulates, a living sculpture responding to the hierarchy of spatial use, the opportunities of sun, air, views, and the shape of the land itself. As with most Blue Sky buildings, wood frame was the construction choice, being relatively lightweight, easy to move, and use. Most of the fir and cedar used in the house is local, harvested and milled on nearby Vancouver Island.

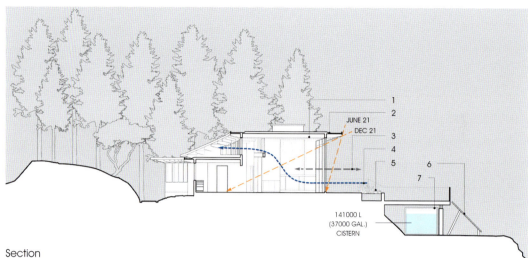

Section

1. Douglas fir timber frame
2. Overhangs minimize summer solar gain and maximize winter solar gain
3. Daylighting and view
4. Natural cross ventilation
5. Vegetable garden
6. Solar photovoltaic panels
7. Rainwater collection to cistern

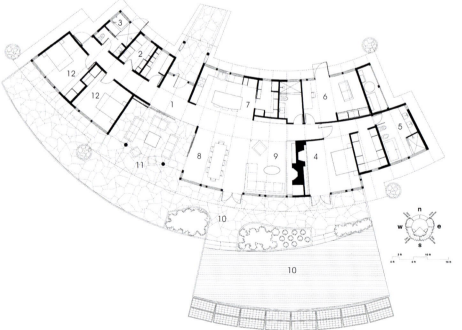

Floor plan
1. Entry
2. Utility/mudroom
3. Powder room
4. Main bedroom
5. En suite
6. Den
7. Kitchen
8. Dining area
9. Living area
10. Terrace
11. Outdoor room
12. Bedroom

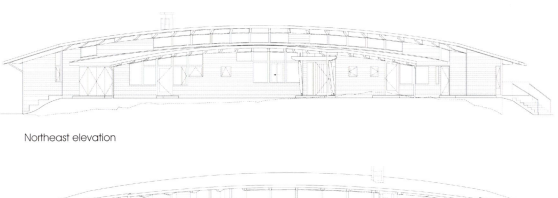

Northeast elevation

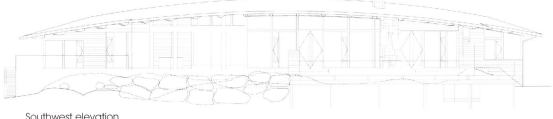

Southwest elevation

RIDGE HOUSE

Salt Spring Island, British Columbia, Canada // Lot area: 9.9 acres; building area: 3,100 sq ft

La casa es la encarnación de los sueños de jubilación de sus propietarios. Después de haber sido propietarios y haber acampado en esta ladera muy arbolada y empinada durante varios años, tuvieron tiempo de formular sus ideas para vivir aquí. La pareja había identificado una estrecha cresta rocosa que discurre aproximadamente de este a oeste a través de un bosquecillo de pequeños madroños retorcidos como su lugar de construcción preferido. La planta y la sección lineal de la Ridge House están determinadas por esta topografía. El ritmo del tejado influye en los ambientes espaciales de las estancias inferiores, ya que pasa de las formas cerradas y protectoras de la entrada a los espacios abiertos y amplios del salón y el comedor. Los detalles sencillos y la cuidadosa artesanía se unen para formar un diseño sofisticado que se posa dramáticamente en su cresta de bosque rocoso.

The house is the embodiment of its owners' retirement dreams. Having owned and camped out at this heavily treed, steep hillside site for several years, they had time to formulate their ideas for living here. The couple had identified a narrow rocky ridge running approximately east-west through a grove of small twisted arbutus trees as their preferred building site. The Ridge House's linear plan and section are determined by this topography. The rhythm of the roof inflects the spatial moods of rooms below as it shifts from the entrance's enclosed and protective forms to open and expansive spaces for the living and dining rooms. Simple details and careful craftsmanship aggregate to form a sophisticated design that perches dramatically on its rocky forest ridge.

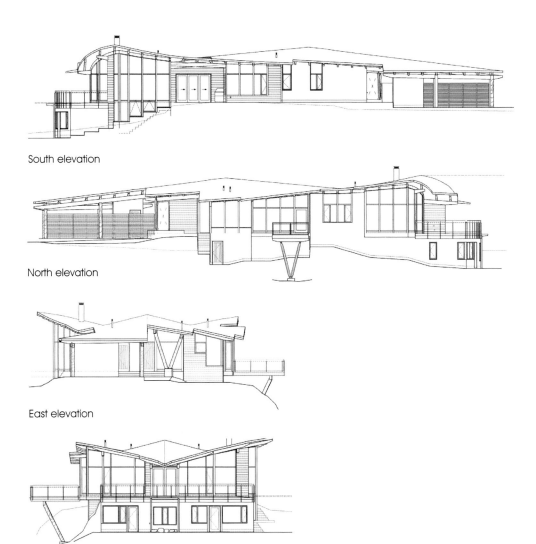

South elevation

North elevation

East elevation

West elevation

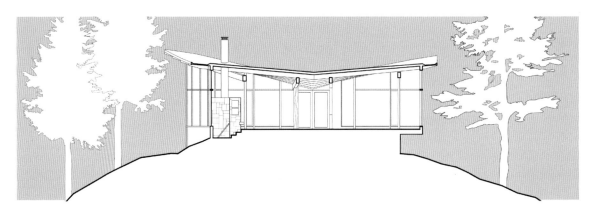

Section

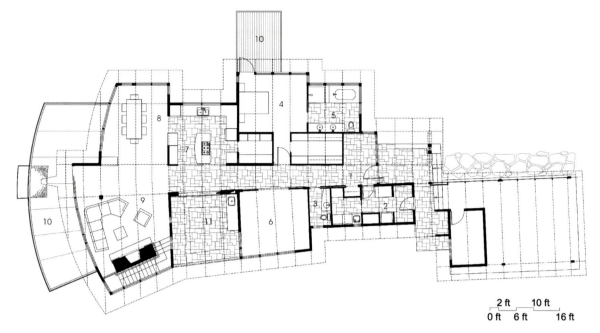

Floor plan

1. Entry
2. Utility/mudroom
3. Powder room
4. Main bedroom
5. En suite
6. Den
7. Kitchen
8. Dining area
9. Living area
10. Terrace
11. Outdoor room

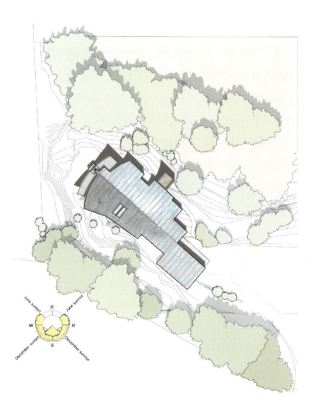

Site plan

CANYON SHELTER

Kittitas County, Washington, United States // Lot area: 12.50 acres; building area: 800 sq ft

El refugio está situado entre un cañón de basalto y una amplia cresta ondulada, creando un puente entre estas dos características paisajísticas distintas. El refugio no es consumido por ninguno de los dos, cómodamente situado en el punto exacto donde las escalas comienzan a cambiar. Es precisamente aquí donde los habitantes pueden ocupar el espacio y al mismo tiempo experimentar la amplia apertura de la cresta. Se trata de un modesto retiro de fin de semana, totalmente desconectado y concebido a partir de tres componentes principales: un largo muro crea un espacio protegido en la cresta del cañón; las terrazas levantan la actividad exterior del suelo rocoso estableciendo un escenario en el paisaje, y el pabellón, que proporciona conexiones visuales con el entorno natural. A lo largo de las estaciones, los habitantes experimentan el refugio y el retiro, pero, al mismo tiempo, la exposición y la conexión con el paisaje occidental.

The shelter is situated between a basalt canyon and a broad rolling ridge, creating a bridge between these two distinct landscape features. The shelter is not consumed by either, comfortably sited at the exact point where scales begin to change. It is precisely here that the inhabitants can occupy the space of the canyon while simultaneously experiencing the broad openness of the ridge. A modest weekend shelter, it is entirely off the grid. It is created from three primary components. A long wall creates a sheltered space on the exposed ridgeline; the terraces lift the outdoor activity off the rocky ground and establish a stage in the landscape; the pavilion provides visual connections with the natural environment. Through the seasons, the inhabitants experience refuge and retreat and, at the same time, exposure and connection to the western landscape.

Environmental elements

BASALT

The Yakima Basalt describes a great series of flood lavas which covered the vast area between what is now the crest of the Cascade Mountains on the west and the mountains of Idaho on the east, and between the mountain of northeastern Washington on the north and the Blue Mountains of Oregon on the South. The age of the Yakima Basalt is late Miocene and early Pliocene. Today, outcroppings of basalt are revealed at fault scarps, ridges, and canyons.

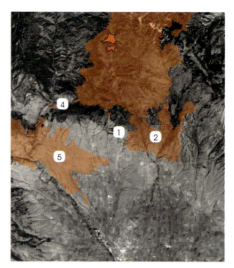

FIRE

With under nine inches of precipitation a year, the shrub-steppe and upland forests of the Kittitas Valley present an extreme fire danger every summer. In the last nine years, fires totaling more than 200,000 acres have scorched the north side of the valley.
1. Site
2. Snag canyon fire - 2014
3. Table mountain fire - 2012
4. Lauderdale fire - 2004
5. Taylor bridge fire - 2012

WIND

Kittitas Valley is aligned between the cool, dense air over the Pacific and the less-dense warmer air of the Columbia Basin and the deserts of Southern Idaho. Westerly flows are compressed over the Cascades, then expand as they spill over the east side. The topography of the valley is nearly perfect for funneling high-speed winds.

Seasonal Change

SPRING

FALL

SUMMER

WINTER

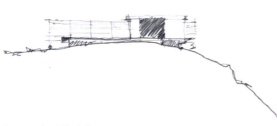

Conceptual Sketch

Section

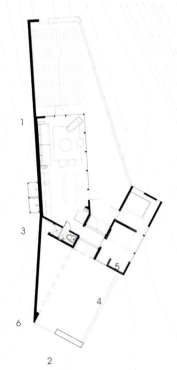

Floor plan

1. Canyon terrace
2. Ridge terrace
3. Pavilion (cooking and living)
4. Bunkroom
5. Bedroom
6. Cisterns
7. Bathroom

ROCKRIDGE

Phoenix, Arizona, United States // Lot area: 37,398 sq ft; building area: 4,951 sq ft

---

Esta residencia se encuentra en un terreno espectacular en la base de la icónica montaña Camelback en Phoenix, Arizona. Los propietarios querían que la propiedad encarnara plenamente la vida al aire libre, aprovechando el clima de «resort» que esta parte del suroeste ofrece la mayor parte del año. Para maximizar el estilo de vida interior/exterior, el diseño tenía como objetivo integrar y capturar los elementos naturales existentes de este magnífico entorno desértico en la experiencia de vida diaria a través de una pared de cristal que se puede ocultar completamente. Frank Lloyd Wright declaró: «Creo que una casa es más un hogar al ser una obra de arte». En el caso de la residencia Rockridge, «la naturaleza es la obra de arte, y nosotros simplemente la capturamos con un recipiente de vidrio funcional que se convirtió en hogar», dice James Trahan, director de 180 Degrees Design + Build.

This residence rests on a spectacular lot at the base of the iconic Camelback Mountain in Phoenix, Arizona. The owners wanted the property to fully embody al fresco living, taking advantage of the "resort" climate this part of the Southwest offers much of the year. To maximize the indoor/outdoor lifestyle, the design aimed at integrating and capturing the existing natural elements of this magnificent desert setting into the daily living experience through a wall of glass that can be completely hidden from sight. Frank Lloyd Wright stated: "I believe a house is more of a home by being a work of art." In the Rockridge residence's case, "nature is the work of art, and we simply captured it with a functional glass vessel that became the home," says James Trahan, Principal at 180 Degrees Design + Build.

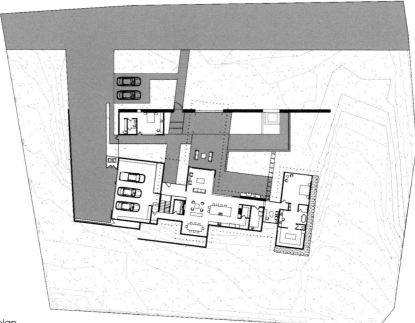

Ground floor plan

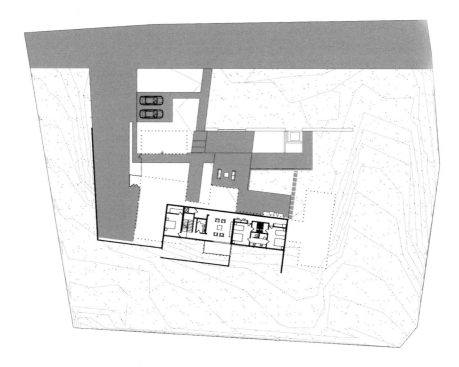

Lower level floor plan

DANCING LIGHT RESIDENCE

Paradise Valley, Arizona, United States // Lot area: 3 acres; main house: 5,700 sq ft; casita: 500 sq ft

---

La casa Dancing Light, de nombre poético, celebra la naturaleza a través de llamativas formas geométricas que reflejan las montañas circundantes y otros detalles, rindiendo homenaje al paisaje del desierto. El elemento más llamativo de toda la estructura, un tejado flotante, aporta un acento escultural al diseño. Al mismo tiempo, crea un equilibrio perfecto entre los acogedores espacios habitables con un techo más bajo y las amplias vistas creadas por los grandes ventanales y el techo elevado. Las formas tectónicas hacen referencia tanto a la geología local como a las formaciones nubosas del monzón. Además de la topografía y las características del terreno, la casa también se inspira en la luz natural. Los muros de tierra apisonada en capas vinculan el moderno interior con el desierto, mientras que el hormigón, el metal y el vidrio proporcionan un contrapeso a las formas orgánicas.

The poetically named Dancing Light house celebrates nature through striking geometric shapes that mirror the surrounding mountains and other details, paying homage to the desert landscape. The eye-catching element of the entire structure, a floating roof canopy, gives a sculptural accent to the design. At the same time, it creates a perfect balance between the cozy living spaces with a lower ceiling and the sweeping views created by the large windows and elevated roof. Tectonic-like shapes reference both the local geology and monsoon cloud formations. Apart from the topography and features of the land, the house also draws inspiration from natural light. Layered rammed-earth walls link the modern interior to the desert, while concrete, metal, and glass provide a counterbalance to the organic forms.

Site plan

1. Foyer
2. Mechanical room
3. Guest bedroom
4. Bathroom
5. Walk-in-closet
6. Garden
7. Storage
8. Terrace
9. Kitchen/great room
10. Master bedroom
11. Master closet
12. Master bathroom
13. Guest house
14. Powder room
15. Office
16. Laundry room
17. Vestibule
18. Four-car garage
19. Pantry
20. Barbecue area
21. Pool
22. Atrium

Contextual illustration

Inspirational imagery

Section A

Section B

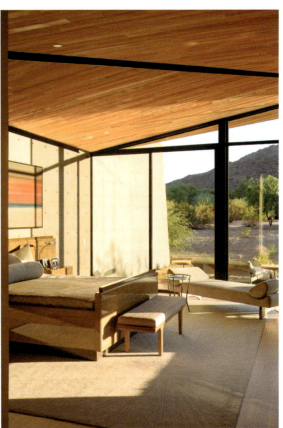

MOD.FAB

Scottsdale, Arizona, United States // Building area: 450 sq ft

Mod.Fab es un ejemplo de vida sencilla, elegante y sostenible a pequeña escala. El prototipo de residencia de un dormitorio se basa en la construcción con paneles para permitir la rapidez y la economía al ser construido bien sobre el terreno o en fábrica y ser, por tanto, transportable. Su chasis se apoya en el suelo en sólo seis puntos, lo que le permite adaptarse a lugares no llanos. El prototipo se construyó en el campus Taliesin West de la Escuela
de Arquitectura Frank Lloyd Wright, en el desierto de Sonora, y desde su finalización, el diseño se ha producido para varios lugares de Estados Unidos y Canadá. Mod.Fab utiliza sistemas de control ambiental pasivos y activos, incluyendo accesorios de bajo consumo, recogida de aguas pluviales, reutilización de aguas grises, ventilación natural, orientación solar y energía fotovoltaica. Mod.Fab fue reconocido como «Proyecto de Arquitectura Verde del Año» por la revista «Time».

The Mod.Fab is an example of simple, elegant, and sustainable living on a small scale. The one-bedroom prototype residence relies on panelized construction to allow for speed and economy on site or in a factory and is transportable via roadway. Its chassis rests on the ground at only six points, allowing it to conform to non-level sites. The prototype was built at the Frank Lloyd Wright School of Architecture's Taliesin West campus in the
Sonoran Desert, and since its completion, the design has been produced for various locations throughout the US and Canada. The Mod.Fab uses a combination of passive and active environmental control systems, including low-consumption fixtures, rainwater harvesting, greywater reuse, natural ventilation, solar orientation, and photovoltaics. The Mod.Fab was recognized as «Green Architecture Project of the Year» by «Time» magazine.

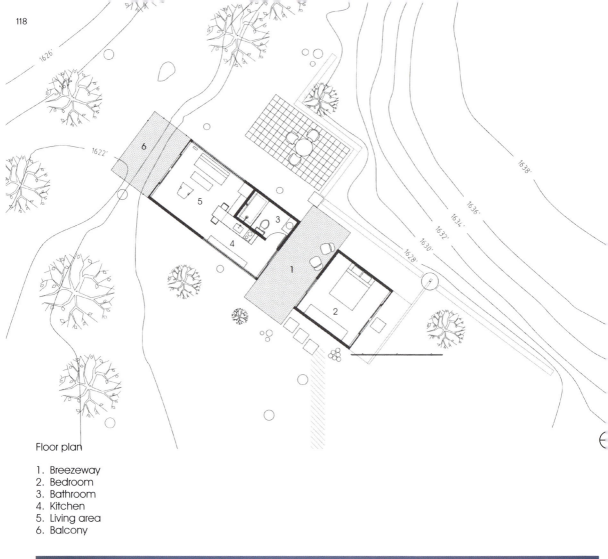

Floor plan

1. Breezeway
2. Bedroom
3. Bathroom
4. Kitchen
5. Living area
6. Balcony

ALTA LUZ

Kendall County, Texas, United States // Lot area: 5 acres; building area: 816 sq ft

Alta Luz es una pequeña casa de un dormitorio situada en una colina con vistas al río Guadalupe, en la región de las colinas de Texas. El lugar está repleto de arbustos de enebro y cedros, que ocultan la casa tanto desde la calle como desde el camino de entrada a la casa. Se utilizaron muros independientes en el paisaje para mantener la casa oculta y dirigir al visitante a través de una procesión de habitaciones exteriores e interiores y una serie de «revelaciones». Uno de estos muros forma la zona de aparcamiento. Oculta la casa a la vista mientras guía al visitante a pie hasta una puerta que revela un espacio exterior que deja ver otro muro en el paisaje, largo, blanco y misterioso. Este «muro independiente» es la propia casa. Uno de los dieciséis paneles idénticos del muro se abre para revelar un volumen interior lleno de luz que, a su vez, deja ver la amplia vista del valle enmarcada por paredes de ventanas colocadas selectivamente.

Alta Luz is a small, one-bedroom house on a hill overlooking the Guadalupe River in the Texas Hill Country. The site is thick with juniper bushes and cedar trees, obscuring the house from the street as well as from the driveway to the house. Freestanding walls in the landscape were used to keep the house obscured and direct the visitor through a procession of outdoor and indoor rooms and a series of "reveals". One of these walls forms the parking area. It hides the house from view as it guides the visitor by foot to a gate that reveals an outdoor space that reveals another wall in the landscape, long, blank and mysterious. This "freestanding wall" is the house itself. One of the wall's sixteen identical wall panels pushes open to reveal a light-filled indoor volume, which in turn, reveals the broad valley view framed by selectively placed window walls.

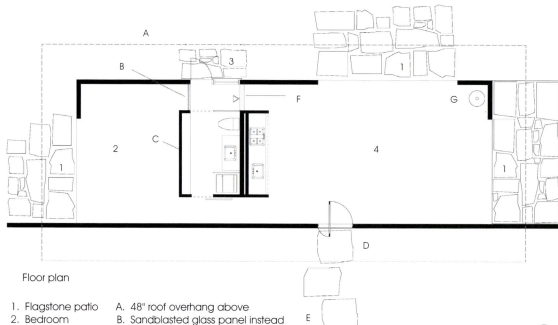

Floor plan

1. Flagstone patio
2. Bedroom
3. Outdoor shower
4. Living area

A. 48" roof overhang above
B. Sandblasted glass panel instead of gypsum wall
C. Walnut paneling on all four sides
D. 4'x8' pivot panel
E. Large flagstones
F. 8'-foot partition
G. Wood stove

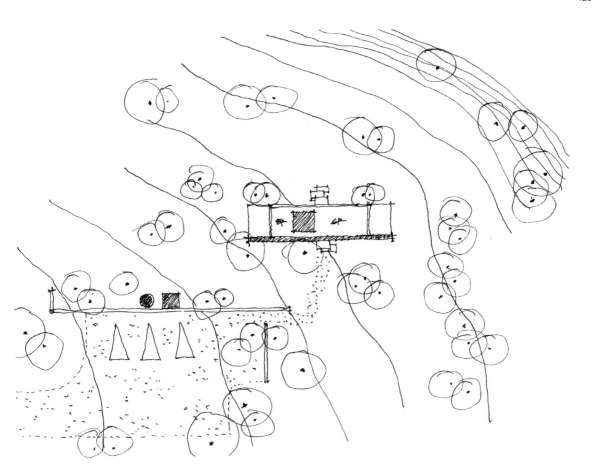

Site plan

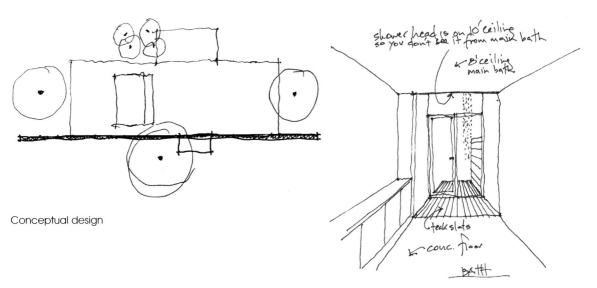

Conceptual design

Bathroom sketch

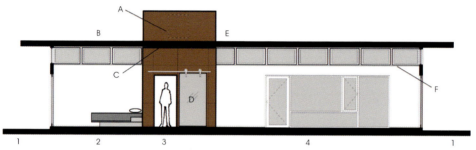

Building secion through hallway

1. Patio
2. Bedroom
3. Bathroom
4. Living area

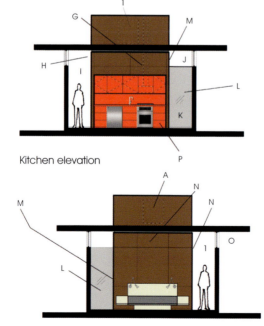

Kitchen elevation

Bedroom elevation

A. A/C compressor inside
B. 6"-thick insulation roof
C. 1/2"x1/2" recess along perimeter of wood core at ceiling
D. Frosted glass rolling door
E. Roof mechanical screen to hide A/C compressor, flues for range, hood, dryer, and plumbing vent
F. 1"x2" wood trim or 1"x8" shelf to run around interior perimeter of the house
G. Range hood and flue hidden inside cabinets
H. Walnut wood panels matching cabinets to wrap around corner and continue down hall to bedroom wall, creating a wood "core" unit
I. Hall open to living area
J. Open to bedroom
K. 42"-deep recess
L. Sandblasted glass panel instead of sheetrock wall
M. Walnut panels to matching cabinets to wrap around corner to 12" recessed wall
N. Walnut panels to wrap around corner from hallway
O. Clerestory window
P. Bold color kitchen recessed into walnut wood core

FRIO RANCH

Real County, Texas, United States // Building area: 3,827 sq ft

Ranch Frio se ajusta al estilo de vida de sus propietarios, que deseaban una casa en la región de las colinas de Texas en un entorno único, donde pudieran recibir a amigos y familiares mientras disfrutaban de las amplias vistas de la colina. Imaginaron una estructura contemporánea y espaciosa que les proporcionara espacio e inspiración para sus esfuerzos artísticos y su trabajo. La paleta de materiales incluye un tejado de metal con juntas alzadas sobre paredes revestidas de madera y metal. En cuanto al espacio, las salas de estar de planta abierta muestran la sencilla pero elegante estructura expuesta y un generoso acristalamiento. La suite principal incluye un gran dormitorio con vistas panorámicas del valle, un baño principal, vestidores y una biblioteca/oficina. En general, el diseño capta la esencia de lo que el propietario quería conseguir, incluyendo comodidad, espacios espectaculares, un aspecto contemporáneo, y todo ello con eficiencia energética.

The Frio Residence fits the lifestyle of its owners, who desired a Texas Hill Country home in a unique setting, where they could entertain friends and family while enjoying the sweeping views from the hilltop location. They envisioned a spacious contemporary structure that would provide space and inspiration for their artistic endeavors and work. The material palette includes standing seam metal roofing above wood and metal-clad walls. Spatially, the open plan living spaces display the simple yet elegant exposed structure and generous glazing. The master suite includes a large bedroom with panoramic views of the valley below, a master bath, walk-in closets, and a library/office area. Overall, the design captures the essence of what the owner sought to achieve, including comfort, dramatic spaces, a contemporary look, and all with energy efficiency.

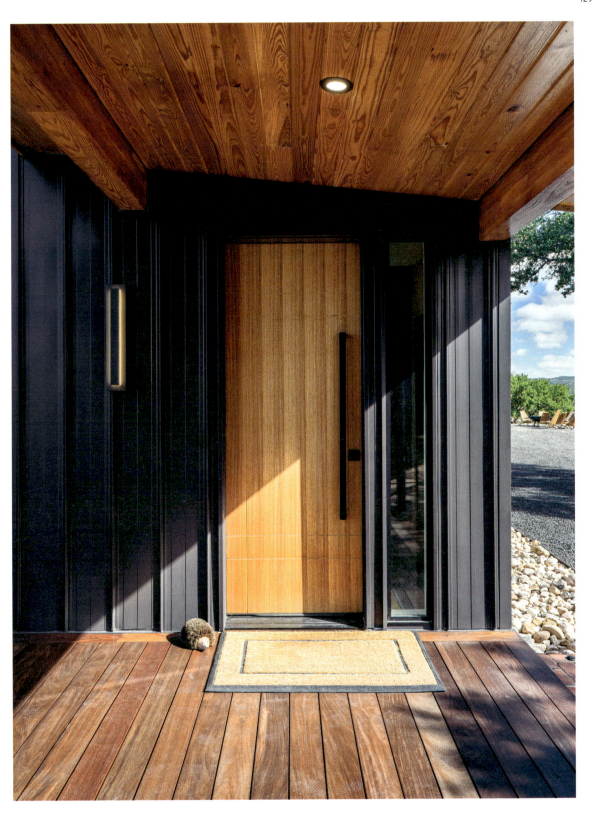

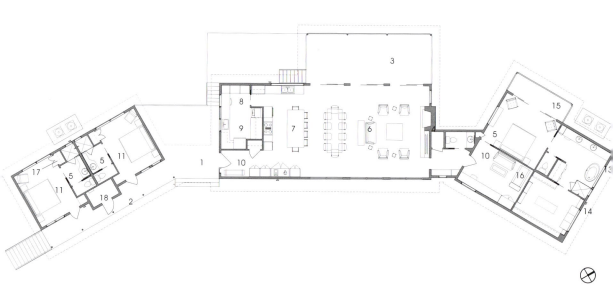

Floor plan

1. Entry porch
2. Porch
3. Main deck
4. Living area
5. Bathroom
6. Dining area
7. Kitchen
8. Pantry
9. Laundry room
10. Hall
11. Bedroom
12. Master bedroom
13. Master bathroom
14. Master closet
15. Master deck
16. Study
17. Closet
18. Storage

CARVE HOUSE

Eugene, Oregon, United States // Lot area: .135 acres; building area: 3,000 sq ft

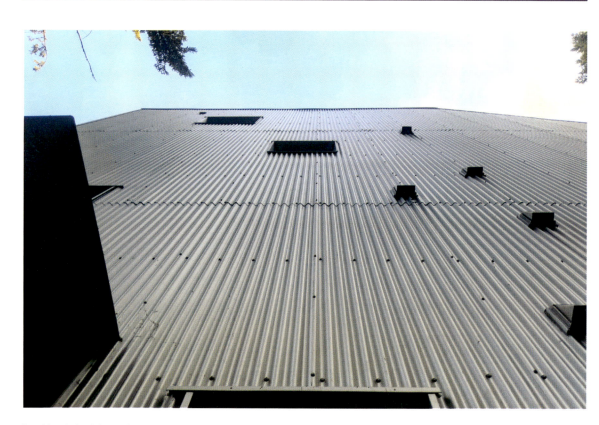

La vista de las lejanas Sisters Mountains y la proximidad a la Universidad de Oregón y a las tiendas de alimentación locales impulsaron este proyecto. La empinada y rocosa ladera orientada al este sugería una torre de cuatro pisos con una huella mínima. El volumen se orientó ampliamente hacia el sur, se talló hasta el nivel del suelo preservando el terreno. Una chimenea solar, suelos radiantes y una estufa de leña calientan la casa durante el invierno. El revestimiento metálico de protección contra la lluvia refleja la luz cambiante. Este exterior rudo y duradero contrasta con un interior cálido y humano, con techos de madera laminada expuesta, suelos de madera blanqueada procedentes del desmonte del terreno y la madera de la entrada que se prolonga hasta la cubierta del tejado, una «habitación al aire libre» entre las copas de los árboles. El emplazamiento está protegido de forma natural de los vientos predominantes del oeste, mientras que el análisis paramétrico se utilizó para aprovechar los beneficios solares a través de las aberturas de las ventanas.

A view of the distant Sisters Mountains and the proximity to the University of Oregon and local food stores drove this project. The steep, rocky east-facing slope suggested a four-story tower with a minimal footprint. The volume was broadly oriented to the south, carved back to the ground level, and preserving the site where it reaches the ground. A solar chimney, radiant floors, and a wood stove heat the house during the winter. Metal rain screen siding reflects the changing light conditions. This gritty, durable exterior contrasts with a warm, human-scaled interior of exposed Glulam ceilings, bleached wood floors from site clearing, and entry wood which continue to the roof deck, an "outdoor room" among the treetops. The site is naturally sheltered from the prevailing western winds, while parametric analysis was used to minimize solar gains through window apertures.

Architect, owner, and builder Philip Speranza

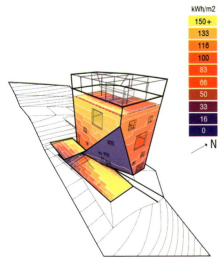

Spring radiation map

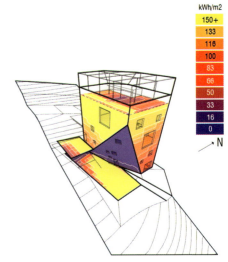

Spring radiation map

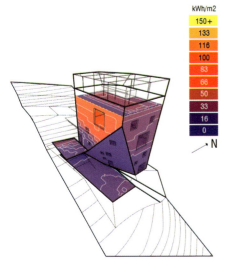

Winter radiation map

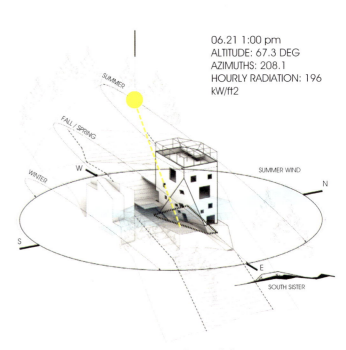

Site and Atmosphere, passive cooling parti diagram

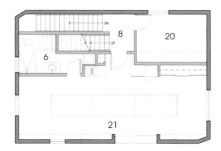

Fourth floor plan

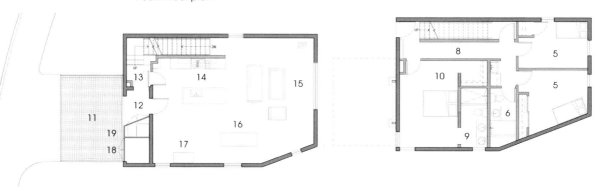

Third floor plan Second floor plan

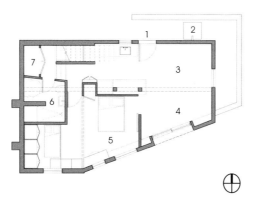

First floor plan

1. Entry
2. Roof water
3. Living area
4. Dining area
5. Bedroom
6. Bathroom
7. Mechanical closet
8. Hallway
9. Master bathroom
10. Master bedroom
11. Bridge
12. Porch
13. Mudroom
14. Kitchen
15. Living area
16. Dining area
17. Study
18. Bike storage
19. Refuse
20. Studio
21. Office

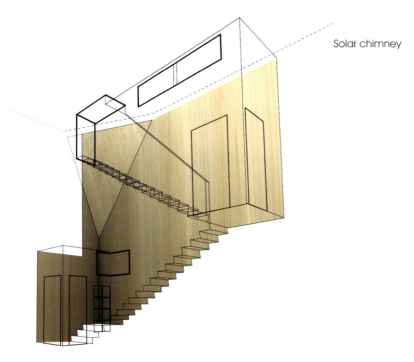
Solar chimney